JESUS
IN THE QURAN

Abd Ar-Rahman bin
Abd Al-Kareem Ash-Sheha

© **Cooperative Office for Islamic Propagation in Rabwah , 1438** *King Fahd National Library Cataloging-in-Publication Data*
Al-Sheha, Abdulrahman bin Abdul Kareem
Jesus in the Quran. / Abdulrahman bin Abdul Kareem Al-Sheha.- Riyadh, 1438

64 p; 15.3 x 19.6 cm
ISBN: 978-603-90936-0-2

1- Jesus Christ in the Quran   I-Title
229.5 dc   1438/6129

L.D. no. 1438/6129
ISBN: 978-603-90936-0-2

In the name of Allah, the Beneficent, the Merciful.

Dear Reader,

Islam is a complete and integral Divine religion and way of life. It has a complete code of ethics for a happy life, as well as a peaceful and tranquil life after death.

Islam is free from all imperfections and defects.

Any deviant or abnormal behavior observed in a Muslim should have no bearing on Islam, none whatsoever.

The reason for such deviant behavior is generally a poor understanding of the faith, and in other cases, weak faith that leads to the person going astray from what is proper and noble.

It is unjust and unreasonable for Islam to be assessed or evaluated based on any individuals' behavior or attitudes, with the exception of the Prophet Muhammad, who is the best example and role model for all humans.

TABLE OF
CONTENTS

FOREWORD

Osoul Center

This book has been conceived, prepared and designed by the Osoul Centre. All photos used in the book belong to the Osoul Centre. The Centre hereby permits all Sunni Muslims to reprint and publish the book in any method and format on condition that 1) acknowledgement of the Osoul Centre is clearly stated on all editions; and 2) no alteration or amendment of the text is introduced without reference to the Osoul Centre. In the case of reprinting this book, the Centre strongly recommends maintaining high quality.

+966 504 442 532

+966 11 445 4900

+966 11 497 0126

P.O.BOX 29465 Riyadh 11457

osoul@rabwah.com

www.osoulcenter.com

All praise be to God, the Lord of all the worlds, the Creator of the heavens and earth and all creatures living in them. May God grant peace and blessings to Prophet Muhammad, God's final Messenger, whose message brought mercy to all mankind. May He also give His blessings to all the prophets and messengers whom He sent to guide mankind out of darkness and into light.

At the Osoul Centre for Islamic Advocacy, every new release that we produce gives us a great opportunity to interact with our readers. All our releases have the same overall objective; to present Islam to mankind, as it truly is. We aim to make people aware of Islam's fine aspects and profound teachings and to show clearly that it is the only faith that provides practical and effective solutions to all the problems faced by humanity. Islam gives clear and solid answers to all of the questions that have troubled people over many generations, such as: How did we come into existence and why do we exist? Where do we go from here? Furthermore, Islam is the only religion that requires its followers to love and respect all the prophets God sent, particularly Moses and Jesus (peace be upon them both).

We take great care to provide solid and rational proofs for our arguments, so as to give our readers the reassurance they need, and our releases also refute the accusations levelled against Islam and provide clarification to people's misunderstandings of Islamic teachings.

By God's grace, Islam is the fastest growing religion in our time, as confirmed by a study undertaken by the Pew Research Center[(1)], and our motive is to make this great divine faith known to all people.

This book, *Jesus in the Qur'an*, speaks first about people's need to receive the divine message through prophets. They need this as much as they need food and drink to survive, if not more. God's messengers and prophets were assigned the task of giving people the right concept of God, their Creator, and explaining to them how to earn His pleasure and acceptance, and how to avoid incurring His anger. They put all this into practice so that their teachings would serve as a code by which to live, setting human life on the right course and ensuring their happiness in the life to come.

The author relates the story of Jesus, son of Mary (peace be upon him), starting at a point well before his birth, when his virtuous mother was pregnant. He then reports the circumstances of his birth and speaks about Jesus's message and the opposition he had to endure. The author then discusses the Qur'anic account of Jesus, which makes clear that he enjoys a very high position with God Almighty.

We hope that readers will find this book useful in adding to their knowledge and understanding of Islam.

Basil ibn Abdullah al-Fawzan
Executive Director

(1) "The Future of the Global Muslim Population", Pew Research Center, 27 January 2011,
    Available at http://goo.gl/uk8y1i

مَا كَانَ مُحَمَّدٌ أَبَا أَحَدٍ مِّن رِّجَالِكُمْ وَلَٰكِن رَّسُولَ اللَّهِ وَخَاتَمَ النَّبِيِّينَ

- "Muhammad is not the father of [any] one of your men, but [he is] the Messenger of Allah and last of the prophets." (Qur'an 33:40)

INTRODUCTION

What are the beliefs of a Muslim in relation to the Prophet Jesus 🕮(1)? Do Muslims actually revere and respect him? Today, the media is responsible for spreading a negative image about Islam, and due to that, Islam appears to be a religion of hate and intolerance to the average person. In reality, anyone who has met a practicing Muslim will know that they are a very peaceful and tolerant people.

The belief system of Islam clearly indicates that it is a religion of tolerance. A key aspect of Islam is a belief in all of the Prophets and Messengers sent by God. Accounts of each of them are detailed in the Qur'an and in Prophetic Traditions. Before delving into the details of the life story of Jesus, I believe it is important to first give a brief introduction to the purpose behind the creation of humankind and the important role spiritual guidance plays in our lives.

In general, spiritual guidance is essential in keeping us balanced in all aspects of our lives. The Qur'an is the divine scripture of Allah(2) revealed to the Prophet Muhammad 🕮 who is the last of all Prophets and Messengers. Due to this fact, certain intrinsic qualities are found in Islam. It is an all-encompassing faith, applicable to people of all times and places. It is applicable to all of humanity's problems. Islam is not simply a religion; rather, it is a complete way of life.

Another intrinsic quality of Islam is that it is a religion of common sense and logic. Take into consideration some of the following examples of Islamic beliefs to clarify this point. As Muslims, we believe that God is the Creator of all and that He has no partner. The Messenger of Islam, Muhammad 🕮, mentioned the stages of creation, as narrated by his companion, Imran bin Husain. He said:
Some people from Yemen came to [the Prophet] and he said, "Accept the good tidings, O people of Yemen, for Bani Tamim refused them." They said, "We accept it, O Allah's Messenger 🕮! We have come to ask you about this matter (the start of creation)." He

---

(1) This symbol means: "May God exalt his mention."

(2) Allah is simply the Arabic word for God, and you will find both terms used interchangeably in this booklet.

said, "First of all, there was nothing but Allah, and then He created His Throne. His throne was over the water, and He wrote everything in the Book and then created the Heavens and the Earth." (Bukhari)

God was always there, unlike His creation, who have a sure beginning. God, the Exalted, says:

"He is the First and the Last, the Ascendant and the One Who has infinite knowledge, and He is, of all things, Knowing." (Qur'an 57:3)

God was the First. Nothing was before Him. He brought all creation into existence. He is unlike any of His creation. There are no similarities between Him and us. God, the Exalted, says:

"There is nothing like unto Him, and He is the Hearing, the Seeing." (Qur'an 42:11)

God has clarified to us that it is impossible for anyone to describe Him, and that no one can encompass His greatness. This alone puts us in awe of God, and affirms our belief in His uniqueness and our need to worship Him alone. God, the Exalted, says:

"Allah knows what is [presently] before them and what will be after them, but they do not encompass it in knowledge."(Qur'an 20:110)

Everything besides God is a created being, brought into existence by God, Himself. He brought forth these creations into existence from mere nothingness. God, the Exalted, says:

"That is Allah, your God, Creator of all things. There is no deity except Him, so how are you deluded?" (Qur'an 40:62)

One of the key beliefs a Muslim adheres to is that Allah creates whatever He wills and does as He pleases. Nothing can withstand the decrees of God. God, the Almighty, says:

"And your Rubb[(1)] creates what He wills and chooses; not for them was the choice. Exalted is Allah and high above what they associate with Him." (Qur'an 28:68)

Allah does not create without purpose; neither would He leave His creation without guidance. No creature has been created in this universe except that behind its creation is a divine wisdom and purpose. At times we know this wisdom, and at times we do not. Modern science in many situations has been successful in deciphering the wisdom behind certain things that may seem to otherwise have no purpose.

God has clarified to us that it is impossible for anyone to describe Him, and that no one can encompass His greatness.

Allah does not create without purpose; neither would He leave His creation without guidance.

(1) There is no proper equivalent for Rubb in the English language. It means the Creator, the Fashioner, the Provider, the One upon Whom all creatures depend for their means of subsistence, and the One Who gives life and causes death.

THE FIRST EVENTS OF CREATION

The Qur'an, which is the word of God, clarifies to us that this world came into existence from mere nothingness. God, the Exalted, says:
"Originator of the heavens and the earth; when He decrees a matter, He only says to it, 'Be,' and it is." (Qur'an 2:117)

The Messenger of God ﷺ clarified to us that the first thing created was water. Water is found in all creation. Allah created this with His power. In the Prophetic Tradition it states:
"Everything is created from water." (Ibn Hibban)

THE CREATION OF THE HEAVENS AND THE EARTH

Allah informs us in the Qur'an that He created the Heavens and the earth in six days. God was not exhausted, nor did He face any difficulty in creating this. He, the Exalted, says:
"And We did certainly create the heavens and earth and what is between them in six days, and there touched Us no weariness." (Qur'an 50:38)

God could easily have created all of this within a mere moment. God, the Exalted, says:
"And to Allah belongs the unseen [aspects] of the heavens and the earth. And the command for the Hour is not but as a glance of the eye or even nearer. Indeed, Allah is over all things competent." (Qur'an 16:77)

If God could have created this in the blink of an eye, why didn't He? Imam Ibn al-Jozi, may God have mercy on him, gave insight into this issue. He said:

01 God demonstrated his infinite wisdom behind creation. Creating all existence quickly would be evident of His power, whereas, creation in a slow manner would be evident of His wisdom.

02 God wanted to show His slaves the importance of being patient.

God created the heavens and earth in six days to show that everything has a set term in life.

Another scholar, Al-Qurtubi, mentioned another reason in relation to this. He said, "God created the heavens and earth in six days to show that everything has a set term in life."

God, the Exalted, says:
"Say, 'Do you indeed disbelieve in He who created the earth in two days and attribute to Him equals? That is the Lord of the worlds.' And He placed on the earth firmly set mountains over its surface, and He blessed it and determined therein its [creatures'] sustenance in four days without distinction - for [the information] of those who ask. Then He directed Himself to the heaven while it was smoke and said to it, and to the earth, 'Come [into being], willingly or by compulsion.' They said, 'We have come willingly.' And He completed them as seven heavens within two days and inspired in each heaven its command. And We adorned the nearest heaven with lamps and as protection. That is the determination of the Exalted in Might, the Knowing." (Qur'an 41:9-12)

This life is not as the atheists assert, without resurrection, accountability or requital. It is only a temporary stage.

Another Islamic scholar said, "The two days in which God created the earth and the two in which He created the mountains and ordained His decrees for each are indeed of His days. Their length is unknown to us, for they are not simple 24 hour intervals as we are accustomed to as humans. These days maybe the periods in which the earth is known to have formed and come into existence. Allah knows best."

THE WISDOM BEHIND THE CREATION OF MAN

Now that we have spoken on the creation of the world, other important questions arise: What is the significance of the creation of man? What is the goal behind this creation? God clarifies this in His words:

"And I did not create the jinn and mankind except to worship Me. I do not want from them any provision, nor do I want them to feed Me. Indeed, it is Allah who is the [continual] Provider, the firm possessor of strength." (Qur'an 51:56-58)

This life is not as the atheists assert, without resurrection, accountability or requital. It is only a temporary stage. God, the Exalted, says:

"And they say, 'There is not but our worldly life; we die and live, and nothing destroys us except time.' And they have of that no knowledge; they are only assuming." (Qur'an 45:24)

How difficult would it be for a person to live his life with no purpose! As any individual is in need of satisfying natural, human desires, they are also in need of spiritual satisfaction as well. This cannot be achieved except if one educates himself about God. Knowledge of God cannot be gathered solely from one's mind or surroundings; one must turn to Divine Scripture. It is important that one understands that the atheistic approach to life is not the result of today's technological advancements. It is a very old belief upheld from time immemorial. It has been handed down throughout the ages by those who have no belief. God, the Exalted, says:

"And We sent among them a messenger from themselves [saying], 'Worship Allah; you have no deity other than Him. Will you not fear Him?' And the eminent among his people who disbelieved and denied the meeting of the Hereafter while We had given them luxury in the worldly life said, 'This is not but a man like yourselves. He eats of that from which you eat and drinks of what you drink. And if you should obey a man like yourselves, indeed, you would then be losers.

Does he promise you that when you have died and become dust and bones that you will be brought forth [once more]? Far-fetched, far-fetched indeed is what you are promised! Life is not but our worldly life - we die and live, but we will not be resurrected.'" (Qur'an 23:32-37)

All of humankind began as one nation, living in one area. But as our numbers increased, we began spreading into different areas.

THE NEED FOR MESSENGERS

Through historical evidence, we know that all of humankind began as one nation, living in one area. But as our numbers increased, we began spreading into different areas. God, the Exalted, says:

"And mankind was only one community [united in religion], but [then] they differed. And if not for a word that preceded from your Rubb, it would have been judged between them [immediately] concerning that over which they differ." (Qur'an 10:19)

The result of moving to different regions of the world led to the formation of traditions and languages that differentiate us from one another today.

The result of moving to different regions of the world led to the formation of traditions and languages that differentiate us from one another today. As creation spread out, God sent to each group of people a prophet to remind them of the message of the belief in the Oneness of God.

Indeed, God is Just. He would never punish a people, except after sending a prophet to clarify the message to them. The Prophets and Messengers warned their people from going astray. No nation of the past was ever left without a warner. God, the Exalted, says:

"Indeed, We have sent you with the truth as a bringer of good tidings and a warner. And there was no nation in the past except that there had passed within it a warner." (Qur'an 35:24)

Allah would send Prophets and Messengers to bring people back to the message of Tawheed (the belief in the Oneness of God). God, the Exalted, says:
"And We certainly sent into every nation a messenger, [saying], 'Worship Allah and avoid Taghut.[1]' And among them were those whom Allah guided, and among them were those upon whom error was [deservedly] decreed. So proceed through the earth and observe how was the end of the deniers." (Qur'an 16:36)

Allah sent these Prophets and Messengers so that no nation would have any excuse against what God ordains for them in the Hereafter. God, the Exalted, says: "[We sent] messengers as bringers of good tidings and warners so that mankind will have no excuse against Allah after the messengers. And ever is Allah Exalted in Might and Wise." (Qur'an 4:165)

All Prophets and Messengers were human beings. They did not innately possess any god-like characteristics or superhuman abilities. God aided them with miracles. God, the Exalted, says:
"And We did not send before you, [O Muhammad], any of the messengers except that they ate food and walked in the markets. And We have made some of you [people] as trial for others - will you have patience? And ever is your Lord, Seeing." (Qur'an 25:20)

Allah clarifies this to ensure that no one would have a doubt about their nature. God, the Almighty, says:
"And We have already sent messengers before you and assigned to them wives and descendants. And it was not for a messenger to come with a sign except by the permission of Allah. For every term is a decree." (Qur'an 13:38)

The Prophets and Messengers had no power to control the affairs of the universe. They had no power even over their own protection. God, the Exalted, says, regarding the Prophets and Messengers:
"Say, 'I hold not for myself [the power of] benefit or harm, except what Allah has willed. And if I knew the unseen, I could have acquired much wealth, and no harm would have touched me. I am not except a warner and a bringer of good tidings to a people who believe.'" (Qur'an 7:188)

(1) The Arabic word taghut refers to idolatry, associating partners with God. This can be anything worshipped other than the one true God.

إِنَّ مَثَلَ عِيسَىٰ عِندَ ٱللَّهِ كَمَثَلِ آدَمَ خَلَقَهُ مِن تُرَابٍ ثُمَّ قَالَ لَهُۥ كُن فَيَكُونُ

- "To God, the case of Jesus is as that of Adam, whom He created from the earth and then said to him, 'Exist,' and Adam came into existence. The truth is from your Lord, so do not be among the doubters." (Qur'an 3:59-63)

THE GREAT PROPHETS OF GOD

All Prophets and Messengers were sent with one Message. God says:
"Or have they taken gods besides Him? Say, [O Muhammad to them], 'Produce your proof. This [Qur'an] is the message for those with me and the message of those before me.' But most of them do not know the truth, so they are turning away. And We sent not before you any messenger except that We revealed to him that, 'There is no deity except Me, so worship Me.'" (Qur'an 21:24-25)

The belief in the Oneness of God was the central message delivered by all Prophets and Messengers to their respective peoples. God, the Exalted, says:
"He has ordained for you of religion what He enjoined upon Noah and that which We have revealed to you, [O Muhammad], and what We enjoined upon Abraham and Moses and Jesus - to establish the religion and not be divided therein. Difficult for those who associate others with Allah is that to which you invite them. Allah chooses for Himself whom He wills and guides to Himself whoever turns back [to Him]." (Qur'an 42:13)

PEOPLES NEED FOR PROPHETS AND MESSENGERS

As we mentioned previously, people are in need of Prophets and Messengers as they are in need of food and drink to sustain themselves. The Scholar Ibn al-Qayyim, may God have mercy on him, said:
"There is no path to happiness and success except through what the Messengers have given us. One would only be able to discern between good and bad through what the Messengers have conveyed to us (in terms of revelation) from God. People of guidance are distinguished by their obedience to the Message. The necessity of knowing the Message is a more pressing need (for man) than finding food and drink. The example of the importance of guidance to mankind is similar to the importance of water to a fish. If taken out of water, it would die. Similarly, no one will truly realize the explicit need of spiritual guidance except one who has a living heart."

THE WISDOM OF GOD IN CHOOSING HIS PROPHETS AND MESSENGERS

The Message and prophethood is a divine gift, which God gives to whomever He pleases. It is not given to one on account of their lineage, authority or position in society. God, the Exalted, says: "Allah chooses from the angels messengers and from the people [as well]. Indeed, Allah is Hearing and Seeing." (Qur'an 22:75)

The Message and prophethood is a divine gift, which God gives to whomever He pleases. It is not given to one on account of their lineage, authority or position in society.

No one should show any jealousy towards the Prophet Muhammad ﷺ for the message he was given. God, the Exalted, says: "Or do they envy people for what Allah has given them of His bounty? But we had already given the family of Abraham the Scripture and wisdom and conferred upon them a great kingdom." (Qur'an 4:54)

The Prophets of God differ in terms of rank and superiority. They are not equal in terms of merit. God, the Exalted, says: "Those messengers - some of them We caused to exceed others. Among them were those to whom Allah spoke, and He raised some of them in degree. And We gave Jesus, the Son of Mary, clear proofs, and We supported him with the Holy Spirit. If Allah had willed, those [generations] succeeding them would not have fought each other after the clear proofs had come to them. But they differed. Some of them believed and some of them disbelieved. And if Allah had willed, they would not have fought each other, but Allah does what He intends." (Qur'an 2:253)

The Prophets of God differ in terms of rank and superiority. They are not equal in terms of merit.

THE CREATION OF ADAM, THE FATHER OF HUMANKIND

Allah has ordained that the ones chosen by Him will inhabit earth. They would work the lands and build thereon. They would be tested in the material realm so it would be established who is obedient and pious, and who is ignoble. God, the Exalted, says: "And [mention, O Muhammad], when your Lord said to the angels, 'Indeed, I will place upon the earth a successive authority.' They said, 'Will You place upon it one who causes corruption therein and sheds blood, while we declare Your praise and sanctify You?' Allah said, 'Indeed, I know that which you do not know.'" (Qur'an 2:30)

The authority God first placed on earth was the Prophet Adam, the father of humankind. God created Adam on a Friday, as is mentioned in the Prophetic Tradition:
"The best day on which the sun has risen is Friday. In it God created Adam, and on it he was admitted into Heaven and on it he was expelled from it, and the Final Hour will be established on a Friday." (Muslim)

For this reason, God chose Friday as the weekly holiday for the Muslims. Due to the lofty status Adam held, Allah ordered the angels to bow down to him out of respect and honor. All of the angels immediately did this. Satan (Iblees), a jinn in the company of the angels, refused to bow down to him. Arrogance and pride prevented him from obeying the command of God. God, the Exalted, says about this:

"[So mention] when your Lord said to the angels, 'Indeed, I am going to create a human being from clay. So when I have proportioned him and breathed into him the soul I created for him, then fall down to him in prostration.' So the angels prostrated - all of them entirely. Except Iblees; he was arrogant and became among the disbelievers. [Allah] said, 'O Iblees, what prevented you from prostrating to that which I created with My hands? Were you arrogant [then], or were you [already] among the haughty?' He said, 'I am better than him. You created me from fire and created him from clay.' [Allah] said, 'Then get out of Paradise, for indeed, you are expelled. And indeed, upon you is My curse until the Day of Recompense.' He said, 'My Lord, then reprieve me until the Day they are resurrected.' [Allah] said, 'So indeed, you are of those reprieved. Until the Day of the time well-known.' [Iblees] said, 'By your might, I will surely mislead them all except, among them, Your chosen servants.' [Allah] said, 'The truth [is My oath], and the truth I say - [That] I will surely fill Hell with you and those of them that follow you all together.'" (Qur'an 38:71-85)

God, through His wisdom, ordained that Adam and his offspring would inhabit the earth. God then created Eve, the wife of Adam.

THE EXPULSION OF ADAM AND HIS WIFE FROM JANNAH

When the Devil refused to bow down before Adam, he sealed his own fate. He informed God that he would mislead the children of Adam and take them with him to the evil abode of Hell. God tells us about this:

"And [mention, O Muhammad], when your Lord said to the angels, 'I will create a human being out of clay from an altered black mud. And when I have proportioned him and breathed into him the soul I created for him, then fall down to him in prostration.' So the angels prostrated - all of them entirely, Except Iblees, he refused to be with those who prostrated. [Allah] said, 'O Iblees, what is [the matter] with you that you are not with those who prostrate?' He said, 'Never would I prostrate to a human whom You created out of clay from an altered black mud.' [Allah] said, 'Then get out of it, for indeed, you are expelled. And indeed, upon you is the curse until the Day of Recompense.' He said, 'My Lord, then reprieve me until the Day they are resurrected.' [Allah] said, 'So indeed, you are of those reprieved. Until the Day of the time well-known.' [Iblees] said, 'My Lord, because You have put me in error, I will surely make [disobedience] attractive to them on earth, and I will mislead them all. Except, among them, Your chosen servants.'" (Qur'an 15:28-40)

> When the Devil refused to bow down before Adam, he sealed his own fate. He informed God that he would mislead the children of Adam and take them with him to the evil abode of Hell.

> The enmity between Adam and Satan (Iblees) began from the beginning of Adam's creation. Iblees lay in wait for him, and tried in every way to make him disobey the commands of Allah.

The enmity between Adam and Iblees began from the beginning of Adam's creation. Iblees lay in wait for him, and tried in every way to make him disobey the commands of Allah. When Iblees realized that God had forbidden Adam from eating from a certain tree, he convinced both Adam and his wife to eat from it. Adam and Eve were then expelled from Heaven. They both repented and were sorrowful for what they did and God accepted their repentance. God, the Exalted, says:

"And [mention] when We said to the angels, 'Prostrate to Adam,' and they prostrated, except Iblees; he refused. So We said, 'O Adam, indeed this is an enemy to you and to your wife. Then let him not remove you from Paradise so you would suffer. Indeed, it is [promised] for you not to be hungry therein or be unclothed. And indeed, you will not be thirsty therein or be hot from the sun.' Then Satan whispered to him. He said, 'O Adam, shall I direct you to the tree of eternity and a kingdom that will not deteriorate?' And Adam and his wife ate of it, and their private parts became apparent to them, and they began to fasten over themselves from the leaves of Heaven. And Adam disobeyed his Lord and erred. Then his Lord chose him and turned to him in forgiveness and guided [him]. [Allah] said, 'Descend from Heaven - all, [your descendants] being enemies to one another. And if there should come to you guidance from Me - then whoever follows My guidance will neither go astray [in the world], nor suffer [in the Hereafter]. And whoever turns away from My remembrance - indeed, he will have a depressed life, and We will gather him on the Day of Resurrection blind.'" (Qur'an 20:116-124)

Once the Devil (Iblees) was cast out of Heaven, and Adam was expelled on account of his disobedience, the progeny of Adam remained obedient to Allah and worshipped Him alone. After ten generations though, people faltered in this regard and went astray. God then sent Prophets and Messengers to guide humankind to the path of God. The first Messenger that God sent after Adam was the Prophet Noah . During his time as a prophet, polytheism had become a norm of life. God, the Exalted, says:

"Noah said, 'My Lord, indeed they have disobeyed me and followed him whose wealth and children will not increase him except in loss. And they conspired an immense conspiracy. And they said, 'Never leave your gods, and never leave Wadd or Suwa' or Yaghuth and Ya'uq and Nasr. And already they have misled many. And, [my Lord], do not increase the wrongdoers except in error.'" (Qur'an 71:21-24)

The best of the Prophets and Messenger are the five known as Ulul'Azm[1], they are:

⓵ THE PROPHET NOAH

He is the first Messenger sent by God. He was sent after his people began practicing Shirk (polytheism). Their condition deteriorated steadily and they forgot the fundamentals of their faith that were passed down to them by their forefathers who upheld the creed of Islam. God, the Exalted, says:

"Indeed, We sent Noah to his people, [saying], 'Warn your people before there comes to them a painful punishment.'" (Qur'an 71:1)

They worshipped five idols named: Wadd, Suwa', Yaghuth, Ya'uq and Nasr. Allah, the Exalted, clarifies their names in the Qur'an saying:

(1) Those of great determination. They are the Messengers of God who exerted great efforts in conveying the Message of God to their peoples.

"And they said, 'Never leave your gods and never leave Wadd or Suwa' or Yaghuth and Ya'uq and Nasr.'" (Qur'an 71:23)

The Prophet Noah was very pious and truthful. He patiently called his people to righteousness. He called on them using a variety of different methods. God, the Exalted, says:

The worst person is he who seeks worldly gain by observing practices which should be done sincerely for the sake of Allah

"He said, 'My Lord, indeed I invited my people [to truth] night and day. But my invitation increased them not except in flight. And indeed, every time I invited them that You may forgive them, they put their fingers in their ears, covered themselves with their garments, persisted, and were arrogant with [great] arrogance. Then I invited them publicly. Then I announced to them and [also] confided to them secretly. And said, 'Ask forgiveness of your Lord. Indeed, He is ever a Perpetual Forgiver.'" (Qur'an 71:5-10)

In spite of his efforts, many of his people turned away and rejected the Message. Only a few followed him and the disbelievers amongst his people continued in their disbelief and evil ways. So Allah prevented them from receiving any rain. Noah informed them that if they were to believe they would receive rain and so they believed, but soon afterward they returned to their disbelief. After spending long years in calling them to the path of Allah, but seeing no answer, he eventually beseeched God, the Exalted, saying:

Innovation in Deen is one of the methods Satan uses to lead people astray.

"And Noah said, 'My Lord, do not leave upon the earth from among the disbelievers an inhabitant. Indeed, if You leave them, they will mislead Your servants and not beget except [every] wicked one and [confirmed] disbeliever.'" (Qur'an 71:26-27)

Allah answered his supplications and He ordered him to build an ark. Noah was a skillful carpenter and those who believed in the Message helped him. Once the ark was complete, God ordered Prophet Noah to gather a pair of each animal (a male and female). God then ordered the heavens to pour rain and the earth to release the water within it. God, the Exalted, says: "The people of Noah denied before them, and they denied Our slave and said, 'A madman,' and he was repelled. So he invoked his Lord, 'Indeed, I am overpowered, so help me.' Then

We opened the gates of the heaven with rain pouring down. And caused the earth to burst with springs, and the waters met for a matter already predestined. And We carried him on a [construction of] planks and nails. Sailing under Our observation as reward for he who had been denied. And We left it as a sign, so is there any who will remember?" (Qur'an 54:9-15)

The Prophet Noah had three offspring: Sam was the father of the Arabs, Ham was the father of the Ethiopians and Yafith was the father of the Europeans.

02 THE PROPHET ABRAHAM (IBRAHIM)

He is known as Khalil ar-Rahman (The Beloved Friend of God). His eldest son was Ismail (Ishmael) and his second son was Ishaq (Isaac), both prophets. From their descendants came the majority of Prophets and Messengers. Allah, the Exalted, says:
"Praise be to Allah, who has granted to me in my old age Ishmael and Isaac. Indeed, my Lord is the Hearer of supplication." (Qur'an 14:39)

Allah chose him to deliver His message. The Prophet Abraham was living in a community of polytheists. They were idolaters who worshipped the stars and hand-made idols. Allah, the Exalted, says:
"And [mention, O Muhammad], when Abraham said to his father Azar, 'Do you take idols as deities? Indeed, I see you and your people to be in manifest error.' And thus did We show Abraham the realm of the heavens and the earth that he would be among the certain [in faith]. So when the night covered him [with darkness], he saw a star. He said, 'This is my lord.' But when it set, he said, 'I like not those that disappear.' And when he saw the moon rising, he said, 'This is my lord.' But when it set, he said, 'Unless my Lord guides me, I will surely be among the people gone astray.' And when he saw the sun rising, he said, 'This is my lord; this is greater.' But when it set, he said, 'O my people, indeed I am free from what you associate with Allah. Indeed, I have turned my face toward He who created the heavens and the earth, inclining toward truth, and I am not of those who associate others with Allah.'" (Qur'an 6:74-79)

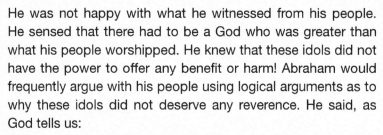

He was not happy with what he witnessed from his people. He sensed that there had to be a God who was greater than what his people worshipped. He knew that these idols did not have the power to offer any benefit or harm! Abraham would frequently argue with his people using logical arguments as to why these idols did not deserve any reverence. He said, as God tells us:

The Prophet Abraham continued calling his people to the path of Allah, to believe in the Oneness of God and to leave aside all that they worshipped. But they rejected his message and even tried to kill him

"And recite to them the news of Abraham, When he said to his father and his people, 'What do you worship?' They said, 'We worship Idols and remain to them devoted.' He said, 'Do they hear you when you supplicate? Or do they benefit you, or do they bring harm?' They said, 'But we found our fathers doing thus.' He said, 'Then do you see what you have been worshipping, You and your ancient forefathers? Indeed, they are enemies to me, except the Lord of the worlds, Who created me, and He [it is who] guides me. And it is He who feeds me and gives me drink. And when I am ill, it is He who cures me. And who will cause me to die and then bring me to life. And who I aspire that He will forgive me my sin on the Day of Recompense.' [And he said], 'My Lord, grant me authority and join me with the righteous.'" (Qur'an 26:69-83)

After continuous preaching, God ordained that the Prophet Abraham take his wife, Hajar, and their son, Ismail, to Makkah. There, God ordained that he build the Ka'bah.

The Prophet Abraham continued calling his people to the path of Allah, to believe in the Oneness of God and to leave aside all that they worshipped. But they rejected his message and even tried to kill him, but Allah saved him. Allah tells us about this, saying:

"He said, 'Then do you worship instead of Allah that which does not benefit you at all or harm you? Uff[(1)] to you and to what you worship instead of Allah. Then will you not use reason?' They said, 'Burn him and support your gods - if you are to act.' Allah said, 'O fire, be coolness and safety upon Abraham.' And they intended for him harm, but We made them the greatest losers." (Qur'an 21: 66-70)

(1)   A word used to express displeasure.

After continuous preaching, God ordained that the Prophet Abraham take his wife, Hajar, and their son, Ismail, to Makkah. There, God ordained that he build the Ka'bah. From the Prophet Ismail's progeny came the final prophet of God, the Prophet Muhammad, who was sent to all of mankind. Allah, the Exalted, says: "And [mention] when Abraham said, 'My Lord, make this a secure city and provide its people with fruits whoever of them believes in Allah and the Last Day.' [Allah] said, 'And whoever disbelieves - I will grant him enjoyment for a little. Then I will force him to the punishment of the Fire, and wretched is the destination.' And [mention] when Abraham was raising the foundations of the House and [with him] Ishmael, [saying], 'Our Lord, accept [this] from us. Indeed You are the Hearing, the Knowing. Our Lord, and make us Muslims [in submission] to You and from our descendants a Muslim nation [in submission] to You. And show us our rites and accept our repentance. Indeed, You are the Accepting of repentance, the Merciful. Our Lord, and send among them a messenger from themselves who will recite to them Your verses and teach them the Book and wisdom and purify them. Indeed, You are the Exalted in Might, the Wise.'" (Qur'an 2:126-129)

03 THE PROPHET MOSES (MUSA)

"And when Moses arrived at Our appointed time and his Lord spoke to him, he said, 'My Lord, show me [Yourself] that I may look at You.' [Allah] said, 'You will not see Me, but look at the mountain. If it should remain in place, then you will see Me.' But when his Lord appeared to the mountain, it was rendered dust, and Moses fell unconscious. And when he awoke, he said, 'Exalted are You! I have repented to You, and I am the first of the believers.'" (Qur'an 7:143)

The Prophet Moses has been mentioned in the Qur'an over 130 times, making him the most mentioned prophet in the Qur'an. God provided him with nine miracles. The first was when his staff was transformed into a serpent, by the will of Allah. The second miracle was when his hand shone forth with a beautiful, radiant light. These signs were granted to Moses so that he could convince Pharaoh of the fallacies of his ways and so that he would accept Islam. Allah, the Exalted, says:

Prophet Moses called the Pharaoh with wisdom and beautiful words to believe in the Oneness of Allah. But the Pharaoh opposed him and gathered together all of the sorcerers of that time to defeat Moses.

"And Moses said, 'O Pharaoh, I am a messenger from the Lord of the worlds. Obligated not to say about Allah except the truth. I have come to you with clear evidence from your Lord, so send with me the Children of Israel.' [Pharaoh] said, 'If you have come with a sign, then bring it forth, if you be of the truthful.' So Moses threw down his staff, and suddenly it was a serpent, manifest. And he drew out his hand; it was white [with radiance] for all to see." (Qur'an 7:104-108)

Allah sent him to the Pharaoh of Egypt and his people to call them to the belief in the Oneness of Allah and to cast aside all of their falsely worshipped gods. God, the Exalted, says:

"And Pharaoh said, 'O eminent ones, I have not known you to have a god other than me. Then ignite for me, O Haman, [a fire] upon the clay and make for me a tower that I may look at the God of Moses. And indeed, I do think he is among the liars.'" (Qur'an 28:38)

The Pharaoh and his people disbelieved in the Message of God, so God punished them with a number of trials.

Prophet Moses called the Pharaoh with wisdom and beautiful words to believe in the Oneness of Allah. But the Pharaoh opposed him and gathered together all of the sorcerers of that time to defeat Moses. Moses, however, was victorious, as his staff transformed, by the will of Allah, into a snake and swallowed the deceptions cast by the sorcerers. Allah mentions this story to us:

"Said the eminent among the people of Pharaoh, 'Indeed, this is a learned magician Who wants to expel you from your land [through magic], so what do you instruct?' They said, 'Postpone [the matter of] him and his brother and send to the cities gatherers who will bring you every learned magician.' And the magicians came to Pharaoh. They said, 'Certainly there is for us a reward if we are the predominant?' He said, "Yes, and moreover you will be among those made near [to me].' They said, 'O Moses, either you throw [your staff], or we will be the ones to throw [first].' He said, 'Throw,' and when they threw, they bewitched the eyes of the people and struck terror into them, and they presented a great [feat of] magic.

And We inspired to Moses, 'Throw your staff,' and at once it devoured what they were falsifying. So the truth was established, and abolished was what they were doing. And Pharaoh and his people were overcome there and became debased. And the magicians fell down in prostration [to Allah]." (Qur'an 7:109-120)

The Pharaoh and his people disbelieved in the Message of God, so God punished them with a number of trials. He sent upon them floods, locusts, lice, frogs, and blood as signs. Still, they refused and persisted in disbelief. Each punishment was lifted by the blessing of the supplication of Prophet Moses. Shortly after each event, they returned and persisted in their disbelief. Allah says about this: "And they said, 'No matter what sign you bring us with which to bewitch us, we will not be believers in you.' So We sent upon them the flood, locusts, lice, frogs and blood as distinct signs, but they were arrogant and were a criminal people. And when the punishment descended upon them, they said, 'O Moses, invoke for us your Lord by what He has promised you. If you [can] remove the punishment from us, we will surely believe you, and we will send with you the Children of Israel.' But when We removed the punishment from them until a term which they were to reach, then at once they broke their word." (Qur'an 7:132-1355)

After all of this, Allah ordered the Prophet Moses to take his people, under the cover of night, and leave Egypt, so that they could practice their faith freely. Once the Pharaoh realized that they had left, he chased after them with his troops. Moses and his people reached the shores of the Red Sea, at which the Children of Israel exclaimed, "The Pharaoh will capture us!" Moses, who had complete trust in God, struck his staff on the water and the sea parted into pathways through which his people entered, by the will of Allah. Allah then saved Moses and his people and destroyed Pharaoh in the sea. God, the Exalted, says:
"And when the two parties saw one another, the companions of Moses said, 'Indeed, we are to be overtaken!' [Moses] said, 'No! Indeed, with me is my Lord; He will guide me.' Then We inspired to Moses, 'Strike with your staff the sea,' and it parted, and each portion was like a great towering mountain. And We advanced thereto the pursuers. And We saved Moses and those with him, all together. Then We drowned the others." (Qur'an 26:61-66)

God, the Exalted, then says:
"And We took the Children of Israel across the sea, and Pharaoh and his soldiers pursued them in tyranny and enmity until, when drowning overtook him, he said,

'I believe that there is no deity except that in whom the Children of Israel believe, and I am of the Muslims.' Now? And you had disobeyed [Him] before and were of the corrupters? So today We will save your body that you may be to those who succeed you a sign. And indeed, many among the people, of Our signs, are heedless." (Qur'an 10:90-92)

Prophet Jesus, the last Prophet from the Children of Israel, has a special place in the hearts of Muslims.

04 THE PROPHET MUHAMMAD ﷺ

The Prophet Muhammad ﷺ is the last of the Prophets and Messengers. He was sent by God to all of mankind. He is from the family of the Prophet Ishmael, the son of Abraham. He was born in Makkah, a few months after the death of his father. His mother later died while he was still young, and he was cared for by his Grandfather, Abdul-Muttalib, and later by his uncle Abu Talib.

Allah has praised Mary, the mother of the Prophet Jesus. Allah describes Mary as pure, chaste and pious.

The Prophet Muhammad ﷺ was a shepherd taking care of a flock of sheep in Makkah. He was very well-known for being trustworthy and having never told a lie in his life. The people of Makkah even called him "The Truthful" and "The Trustworthy". Whenever people left for a trip, they would entrust him with their valuables.

When he reached the age of 40, God sent the Angel Gabriel to him and appointed Muhammad as a Prophet and Messenger to mankind. He spent 13 years in Makkah calling people to the path of God and later on migrated to Madinah. The people of Madinah responded and accepted Islam in droves. He died when he was 63 years old. His followers then spread the Message of Islam across the world, and until today people are accepting Islam in large numbers across the globe.[1]

(1) For more information on the Prophet Muhammad ﷺ, refer to the book, Muhammad, the Messenger of Allah, published by Osoul Center.

05 JESUS, THE MESSENGER OF GOD

Family of Imran

Prophets and Messengers were sent by God continuously after the Prophet Noah, may God praise him. God, the Exalted, says:
"Muhammad is not the father of [any] one of your men, but [he is] the Messenger of God and last of the prophets. And ever is God, of all things, Knowing." (Qur'an 33:40)

The Prophet Jesus, the last Prophet from the Children of Israel, has a special place in the hearts of Muslims. He informed his people of the advent of Prophet Muhammad and he is mentioned in the Qur'an 25 times.

God has conveyed to us in the Qur'an some of the original passages that He revealed to Jesus. God also mentions details about the life of Mary, the mother of Jesus. She is spoken of highly and is known for being pure and chaste. God, the Exalted, says:
"Indeed, God chose Adam and Noah and the family of Abraham and the family of 'Imran over the worlds. Descendants, some of them from others. And God is Hearing and Knowing." (Qur'an 3:33-34)

Mary, may God praise her

God has praised Mary, the mother of the Prophet Jesus. God describes Maryam as pure, chaste and pious. He, the Exalted, says:
"And [the example of] Mary, the daughter of 'Imran, who guarded her chastity, so We blew into [her garment] through Our angel, and she believed in the words of her Lord and His scriptures and was of the devoutly obedient." (Qur'an 66:12)

The Qur'an clarifies that the birth of Mary was the result of a supplication that her own mother made. God, the Exalted, says:
"[Mention, O Muhammad], when the wife of 'Imran said, 'My Lord, indeed I have pledged to You what is in my womb, consecrated [for Your service], so accept this from me. Indeed, You are the Hearing, the Knowing.'" (Qur'an 3:35)

This supplication was the indirect cause through which she and her offspring were protected by God from the Devil. God provided for Mary and reared her with His blessings. Allah says: "But when she delivered her, she said, 'My Lord, I have delivered a female.' And God was most aware of what she delivered, indeed the male is not like the female. 'And I have named her Mary, and I seek refuge for her in You and [for] her descendants from Satan, the expelled [from the mercy of God].' So her Lord accepted her with good acceptance, caused her to grow in a good manner and put her in the care of Zechariah. Every time Zechariah entered upon her in the prayer chamber, he found with her provision. He said, 'O Mary, from where is this [coming] to you?' She said, 'It is from God. Indeed, God provides for whom He wills without account.'" (Qur'an 3:36-37)

Mary was very pious in her worship of God. She was the best of women in her generation.

The birth of the Prophet Jesus was a miracle. Even though Jesus was born to a virgin, he does not deserve, nor require, any worship.

Mary was very pious in her worship of God. She was the best of women in her generation. The Prophet, may God praise him, said:

"From among the women of the world who have reached perfection and who are worthy of following are: Mary, the daughter of Imrân; Khadijah, the daughter of Khuwaylid; Fatima, the daughter of Muhammed and Asiyah, the wife of Pharaoh." (Tirmidhi).

God, the Exalted, says:

"And [mention] when the angels said, 'O Mary, indeed God has chosen you and purified you and chosen you above the women of the worlds. O Mary, be devoutly obedient to your Lord and prostrate and bow with those who bow [in prayer].'" (Qur'an 3:42-43)

God revealed an entire chapter in the Qur'an carrying her name. It is the 19th chapter in the Qur'an. It is the only chapter in the Qur'an named after a woman, and in it God praises Mary. A praise of a similar nature cannot be found in any of the previous Scriptures.

THE PROPHET JESUS

God gave the good news to Mary about Prophet Jesus, may God praise him. God, the Exalted, says:

"[And mention] when the angels said, 'O Mary, indeed Allah gives you good tidings of a word from Him, whose name will be the Messiah, Jesus, the son of Mary - distinguished in this world and the Hereafter and among those brought near [to God]. He will speak to the people in the cradle and in maturity and will be of the righteous.' She said, 'My Lord, how will I have a child when no man has touched me?' [The angel] said, 'Such is God; He creates what He wills. When He decrees a matter, He only says to it, 'Be,' and it is. And He will teach him writing and wisdom and the Torah and the Gospel.'" (Qur'an 3:45-48)

HIS BIRTH:

The birth of the Prophet Jesus was a miracle. Even though Jesus was born to a virgin, he does not deserve, nor require, any worship. Had Jesus deserved any worship on account of his miraculous birth, the Prophet Adam would be more deserving of it than him, since he was created without a father or a mother. Allah, the Exalted, says:

"To God, the case of Jesus is as that of Adam, whom He created from dust and then said, 'Exist,' and Adam came into existence. The truth is from your Lord, so do not be among the doubters." (Qur'an 3:59-60)

- "The Messiah, son of Mary, was only a messenger. [Other] messengers have passed on before him." (Qur'an 5:75)

Allah created and fashioned Jesus as He has all creation. God speaks of the entire ordeal of the birth of Jesus in the Qur'an, saying:

The Qur'an states clearly that Jesus was a man who was chosen by God to convey the message of the belief in the Oneness of God to his people.

People throughout the ages have claimed that God had a child. The polytheists among the Arabs claimed that God had married from the Jinn and that the Angels were His daughters.

"And mention, [O Muhammad], in the Book [the story of] Mary, when she withdrew from her family to a place toward the east. And she took, in seclusion from them, a screen. Then We sent to her Our Angel, and he represented himself to her as a well-proportioned man. She said, 'Indeed, I seek refuge in the Most Merciful from you, [so leave me], if you fear God.' He said, 'I am only the messenger of your Lord to give you [news of] a pure boy.' She said, 'How can I have a boy while no man has touched me and I have not been unchaste?' He said, 'Thus [it will be]. Your Lord says, 'It is easy for Me, and We will make him a sign to the people and a mercy from Us. And it is a matter [already] decreed.' So she conceived him, and she withdrew with him to a remote place. And the pains of childbirth drove her to the trunk of a palm tree. She said, 'Oh, I wish I had died before this and was in oblivion, forgotten.' But he called her from below her, 'Do not grieve. Your Lord has provided beneath you a stream. And shake toward you the trunk of the palm tree. It will drop upon you ripe, fresh dates. So eat and drink and be contented. And if you see from among humanity anyone, say, 'Indeed, I have vowed to the Most Merciful a fast, so I will not speak today to any man.' Then she brought him to her people, carrying him. They said, 'O Mary, you have certainly done a thing unprecedented. O sister of Aaron, your father was not a man of evil, nor was your mother unchaste.' So she pointed to him. They said, 'How can we speak to one who is in the cradle, a baby?' [Jesus] said, 'Indeed, I am the servant of God. He has given me the Scripture and made me a prophet. And He has made me blessed wherever I am and has enjoined upon me prayer and Zakah (charity) as long as I remain alive. And [made me] dutiful to my mother, and He has not made me a wretched tyrant. And peace is on me the day I was born and the day I will die and the day I am raised alive.' That is Jesus, the son of

Mary - the word of truth about which they are in dispute. It is not [befitting] for God to take a son; exalted is He! When He decrees an affair, He only says to it, 'Be,' and it is." (Qur'an 19:16-35)

Allah, the Exalted, says:
"And [mention] the one who guarded her chastity, so We blew into her [garment] through Our angel [Gabriel], and We made her and her son a sign for the worlds." (Qur'an 21:91)

02 THE HUMAN NATURE OF JESUS

The Qur'an states clearly that Jesus was a man who was chosen by God to convey the message of the belief in the Oneness of God to his people. Allah, the Exalted, says:
"The Messiah, son of Mary, was only a messenger. [Other] messengers have passed on before him. And his mother was a supporter of truth. They both used to eat food. Look how We make clear to them the signs, then look how they are deluded." (Qur'an 5:75)

It is not befitting of God to have a wife or children. Alleging that He has a child is indeed a major sin. God, the Exalted, says:
"And they say, 'The Most Merciful has taken [for Himself] a son.' You have alleged an atrocious thing. The heavens almost rupture there from, the earth would split open and the mountains are ready to collapse in devastation. That they attribute to the Most Merciful a son. And it is not fitting for the Most Merciful that He should take a son. There is no one in the heavens and earth, except that he comes to the Most Merciful as a servant." (Qur'an 19:88-93)

A child is the product of two equals coming together. Nothing is like unto God. He has no equal and He has no partners. God, the Exalted, says:
"Say, 'He is Allah, [who is] One. Allah, the Eternal Refuge. He neither begets, nor is he born, nor is there to Him any equivalent.'" (Qur'an Chapter 112)

People throughout the ages have claimed that God had a child. The polytheists among the Arabs claimed that God had married from the Jinn and that the Angels were His daughters. God, the Exalted, says:
"So inquire of them, [O Muhammad], 'Does your Lord have daughters while they

have sons? Or did We create the angels as females while they were witnesses?' Unquestionably, it is out of their [invented] falsehood that they say, 'God has begotten,' and indeed, they are liars. Has He chosen daughters over sons? What is [wrong] with you? How do you make judgment? Then will you not be reminded? Or do you have a clear authority? Then produce your scripture, if you should be truthful. And they have claimed between Him and the jinn a lineage, but the jinn have already known that they [who made such claims] will be brought to [punishment]. Exalted is God above what they describe, except the chosen servants of God [who do not share in that sin]." (Qur'an 37: 149-160)

The Qur'an mentions many intellectual evidences that clearly demonstrate that God is the only One worthy of worship.

Both the Jews and the Christians made similar claims. God, the Exalted, says:

"The Jews say, 'Ezra is the son of God,' and the Christians say, 'The Messiah is the son of God.' That is their statement from their mouths by which they imitate the saying of those who disbelieved [before them]. May God destroy them; how are they deluded? They have taken their scholars and monks as lords besides God, and [also] the Messiah, the son of Mary. And they were not commanded except to worship one God; there is no deity except Him. Exalted is He above whatever they associate with Him." (Qur'an 9:30-1)

Every Muslim believes that all of the prophets and messengers did their duty in conveying to their people the message of belief in the Oneness of God.

The Qur'an clearly states that anyone who believes that Jesus is God, or the son of God, or part of a Trinity, would have embraced a belief that contradicts the Message of Jesus, and thus would be a disbeliever in his Message. The Qur'an clarifies that the message of Jesus was the belief in the Oneness of God. God, the Exalted, says:

"They have certainly disbelieved, those who say, 'God is the Messiah, the son of Mary,' while the Messiah has said, 'O Children of Israel, worship God, my Lord and your Lord.' Indeed, he who associates others with God - God has forbidden him Paradise, and his refuge is the Fire. And there are not for the wrongdoers any helpers. They have certainly disbelieved, those who say, 'God is the third of three.' And there is no god except one God. And if they do not desist from what they are saying, there will surely afflict the disbelievers among them a painful punishment. So will they not repent to God and seek His forgiveness? And God is Forgiving and Merciful." (Qur'an 5:72-74)

The Qur'an mentions many intellectual evidences that clearly demonstrate that God is the only One worthy of worship. He does as He wills and pleases. It also clarifies that all the miracles that happened through Jesus were by the will of God. Jesus himself does not have the power to protect himself from the decrees of God. God, the Exalted, says:
"They have certainly disbelieved, those who say that God is the Messiah, the son of Mary. Say, 'Then who could prevent God at all if He had intended to destroy the Messiah, the son of Mary, or his mother or everyone on the earth?' And to God belongs the dominion of the heavens and the earth and whatever is between them. He creates what He wills, and God is over all things competent." (Qur'an 5:17)

God warns the Jews and Christians not to adulate their Prophets and not to speak in their regard without knowledge. It also goes to tell us that Jesus is only a human being. God, the Exalted, says:
"O People of the Scripture, do not commit excess in your religion or say about God except the truth. The Messiah, Jesus, the son of Mary, was but a messenger of God and His word which He directed to Mary and a soul [created at a command] from Him. So believe in God and His messengers. And do not say, 'Three'. Desist - it is better for you. Indeed, God is only one. Exalted is He above having a son. To Him belongs whatever is in the heavens and whatever is on the earth. And sufficient is God as Disposer of affairs. Never would the Messiah disdain to be a servant of God, nor would the angels near [to Him]. And whoever disdains His worship and is arrogant - He will gather them to Himself all together. And as for those who believed and did righteous deeds, He will give them in full their rewards and grant them extra from His bounty. But as for those who disdained and were arrogant, He will punish them with a painful punishment, and they will not find for themselves besides God any protector or helper." (Qur'an 4:171-173)

03 THE PROPHETHOOD OF JESUS

Every Muslim believes that all of the prophets and messengers did their duty in conveying to their people the message of belief in the Oneness of God. A Muslim is to love and revere all of them as well. We are also ordered by God to defend all of them. God, the Exalted, says:

Before the advent of Prophet Moses, the children of Israel were belittled and forced into menial and harsh labor work.

"Say, [O believers], 'We have believed in God and what has been revealed to us and what has been revealed to Abraham and Ishmael and Isaac and Jacob and the Descendants, and what was given to Moses and Jesus, and what was given to the prophets from their Lord. We make no distinction between any of them, and we are Muslims [in submission] to Him.' So if they believe in the same as you believe in, then they have been [rightly] guided. But if they turn away, they are only in dissension, and God will be sufficient for you against them. And He is the Hearing, the Knowing." ((Qur'an 2:137-138)

The Prophet Jesus took the lead and called the children of Israel to the belief in the Oneness of God and to worship God alone.

Before the advent of Prophet Moses, the children of Israel were belittled and forced into menial and harsh labor work. God, the Exalted, says:

"And [recall, O Children of Israel], when We saved you from the people of Pharaoh, [who were] afflicting you with the worst torment - killing your sons and keeping your women alive. And in that was a great trial from your Lord." (Qur'an 7:141)

God then blessed them with the Prophet Moses, and their condition changed from bad to good. God, the Exalted, says:

"And We caused the people who had been oppressed to inherit the eastern regions of the land and the western ones, which We had blessed. And the good word of your Lord was fulfilled for the Children of Israel because of what they had patiently endured. And We destroyed [all] that Pharaoh and his people were producing and what they had been building." (Qur'an 7:137)

After that, the Children of Israel drifted from the path of God, so God sent them the Prophet Jesus to guide them back to the Straight Path. God, the Exalted, says:

"And We sent, following in their footsteps, Jesus, the son of Mary, confirming that which came before him in the Torah. And We gave him the Gospel, in which was guidance and light and confirming that which preceded it of the Torah as guidance and instruction for the righteous." (Qur'an 5:46)

The Prophet Jesus took the lead and called the children of Israel to the belief in the Oneness of God and to worship God alone and that they uphold the commandments in the Gospel. God, the Exalted, says:
"And when Jesus brought clear proofs, he said, 'I have come to you with wisdom and to make clear to you some of that over which you differ, so fear God and obey me. Indeed, God is my Lord and your Lord, so worship Him. This is the straight path.'" (Qur'an 43:63-64)

When the Prophet Jesus saw that they had disbelieved and rejected the truth, and that they were persistent in their disbelief, He called out to those who believed amongst his people - the disciples. They answered his call and pledged their support. God, the Exalted, says:
"But when Jesus felt [persistence in] disbelief from them, he said, 'Who are my supporters for [the cause of] God?' The disciples said, 'We are supporters for the sake of God. We have believed in God and testify that we are Muslims [submitting to Him]. Our Lord, we have believed in what You revealed and have followed the messenger Jesus, so record us among the witnesses [to truth].'" (Qur'an 3:52-53)

THE DESCRIPTION OF THE PROPHET JESUS

The Qur'an has given us a description of the Prophet Jesus, may God praise him. This description covers some of his mannerisms and also the nature of His message. God mentions that He protected Jesus. God, the Exalted, says:
"And We did certainly give Moses the Torah and followed up after him with messengers. And We gave Jesus, the son of Mary, clear proofs and supported him with the Holy Spirit. But is it not that every time a messenger came to you, [O Children of Israel], with what your souls did not desire, you were arrogant? And a party [of messengers] you denied and another party you killed." (Qur'an 2:87)

God also describes Jesus as being a perfect example in terms of complete faith and sincerity to God. Muslims believe that Prophet Jesus will descend to the earth towards the end of time. God, the Exalted, says:

"Jesus was only a servant upon whom We bestowed favor, and We made him an example for the Children of Israel. And if We willed, We could have made [instead] of you angels succeeding one another on the earth. And indeed, Jesus will be [a sign for] knowledge of the Hour, so be not in doubt of it, and follow Me. This is a straight path." (Qur'an 43:59-61)

The Prophet clarified that one's faith would not be complete unless they believe in Jesus being a Messenger of God.

05 PHYSICAL CHARACTERISTICS OF JESUS

As for his physical qualities and features, the Prophet Muhammad ﷺ described him saying:

"While I was circumambulating the Ka`bah in my dream, suddenly I saw a man of brown complexion and lank hair walking between two men, and water was dripping from his head. I asked, 'Who is this?' The people said, 'He is the son of Mary.'" (Bukhari)

The Prophet ﷺ said:

"The Prophets are brothers from different mothers. The creed they all carry is one, though the specifics of their laws differ. There is no Prophet between Jesus and I. He will break the cross, kill the swine and remove the Jizyah (head tax). He will unite all under one belief and only Islam will prevail during his reign. During his reign, the anti-Christ will be killed and safety and security will spread throughout the lands till animals will harmoniously coexist with each other. Children will play with snakes, not being harmed by them. He will rule amongst the Muslims for as long as Allah wills and then he will die and the Muslims will bury him." (Ahmed)

The Prophet clarified to us that the return of Jesus to the Earth is one of the Final signs of the coming of the Day of Judgment.

The Prophet ﷺ said:

"I saw Jesus, Moses and Abraham. As for Jesus, he has a hue that inclined to pink and he has a broad chest." (Bukhari)

The Prophet clarified that one's faith would not be complete unless they believe in Jesus being a Messenger of God. This would lead one to a blissful life in the Heavenly Abode. The Prophet ﷺ said:

"Whoever testifies that there is no God but Allah, alone without any partners, and that Muhammad is His servant and His Messenger, and that Jesus is the servant of Allah, son of His female servant, His word which He bestowed upon Mary, and a spirit from Him, and that Paradise is true and Hellfire is true, then Allah will admit him into any of the eight gates of Paradise he wishes." (Muslim)

Believing that Jesus is a messenger of God will also increase one's rewards. The Prophet ﷺ said:
"Whoever believes in Jesus the son of Mary as a Prophet and Messenger of God and then believes in me, will have two rewards." (Bukhari)

JESUS AND THE ANTI-CHRIST

The Prophet clarified to us that the return of Jesus to the Earth is one of the Final signs of the coming of the Day of Judgment. The proof of this is in the words of Allah, the Exalted:
"Jesus was only a servant upon whom We bestowed favor, and We made him an example for the Children of Israel. And if We willed, We could have made [instead] of you angels succeeding one another on the earth. And indeed, Jesus will be [a sign for] knowledge of the Hour, so be not in doubt of it, and follow Me. This is a straight path." (Qur'an 43:59-61)

Due to the greatness of the Prophet Jesus, he will be the one who will slay the Anti-Christ. He will also spread the message of Islam during the times of great tribulation. During that time, the good will be viewed as bad and the bad as good. The Prophet ﷺ said:
"O people, there has been no Fitnah (trial) greater on this earth from the time that Adam was created till the end of time than that of the Dajjal (Anti-Christ). Every Prophet warned his people of this trial. I am the last of the Prophets and you are the last of nations, and he will come forth during this era without a doubt. If he comes out while I am among you, I will defend every Muslim. But if he comes out after I pass away, then every Muslim will have to defend himself. And Allah will protect the Muslims after me. He will first emerge from an area between the Greater Syria Area and Iraq. He will go to the east and the west causing problems wherever he goes. O slaves of Allah, O people, be firm! I will describe him to you like no prophet has described him.

He will claim to be your God, but you shall not see God in this world. He is one eyed and your God is not one eyed! It is written between his eyes, 'disbeliever'. Every believer will be able to read it whether they are literate or not. He will have a heaven and a hell with him. His hell is a heaven and the heaven is a hell. Whoever is tried through his hell; let them seek refuge in Allah and recite the first verses of the chapter of al-Kahf.

Due to the greatness of the Prophet Jesus, he will be the one who will slay the Anti-Christ. He will also spread the message of Islam during the times of great tribulation.

He would say to one Bedouin, 'If you see that I resurrect your mother and your father, would you believe in me?' The Bedouin would say yes, and two devils would emerge in the form of his parents and say to him, 'O our son, follow him, for he is your Lord.'

And from his trials, he will kill a person cutting him in half with a saw and then say, 'Look at my slave, I have cut him in half and I shall resurrect him, but he will deny that I am his Lord.' Then Allah would allow him to be resurrected, and the Liar would then ask that person, 'Who is your Lord?' The man who was just cut would say, 'Allah! And you are the enemy of Allah! You are the Anti-Christ! I am now surer than ever that you are the one whom our Prophet warned us against!'

And from his trials, he would order the heavens to pour rain and it would rain. And he would order the earth to bring forth vegetation, and it would do so.

And from his trials, he would pass by a district who disbelieve in him, and he would order the land to stop producing its vegetation and all their herds would die... and he would pass by another and ask them to believe in him and they would, and he would order the sky to rain and it would, and he would order the earth to bring forth vegetation and it would and their flocks will return from grazing fatter than they have ever been, with their flanks stretched and their udders full.

He will go to every corner of this world except for Makkah and Madinah. At every tunnel and gate, he will be met by Angels standing guard with swords unsheathed.

He will go to every corner of this world except for Makkah and Madinah. At every tunnel and gate, he will be met by Angels standing guard with swords unsheathed. Until he reaches al-

Zarib al-Ahmar and camps at the edge of the salt-marsh, then Madinah would shake violently three times and all the hypocrites would exit and go out to join him, and it will be cleansed of evil, in the same way that the bellows cleanses off the dross of iron. That day will be called Yawm al-Khalas (The Day of Purification).

It was said, 'Where are the Arabs on that day?' He said, they would be few in number. Most of them will be in Jerusalem, and their Imam will be a righteous man. Whilst their Imam is going forward to lead the people in praying the Morning Prayer, Jesus the son of Mary will descend.

The Imam will step back, to let Jesus lead the people in prayer, but Jesus will place his hand between the man's shoulders and say, 'Go forward and lead the prayer, for the Iqamah was made for you. So the Imam will lead the people in prayer, and afterwards Jesus will say, 'Open the gate. The gate will be opened, and behind it will be the Anti-Christ and seventy thousand Jews, each of them bearing a sword and shield. When the Anti-Christ sees Jesus, he will begin to dissolve like salt in water, and he will try to escape...

Jesus the son of Mary will be a just administrator and leader of my Ummah. He will break the cross, kill the pigs, and abolish the Jizyah (tax on non-Muslims). He will not collect the (charity) Sadaqah, so he will not collect sheep and camels. Mutual enmity and hatred will disappear. Every harmful animal will be made harmless, so that a small boy will be able to put his hand into a snake's mouth without being harmed, and a small girl will annoy a lion without him harming her, and a wolf will go among sheep as if he were a sheepdog.

The earth will be filled with peace as a container is filled with water. People will be in complete agreement, and only Allah will be worshipped. Wars will cease, and the authority of Quraysh will be taken away. The earth will be like a silver basin, and will produce fruits so abundantly that a group of people will gather to eat a bunch of grapes and be satisfied by it, and another group will gather to eat one pomegranate and will be satisfied. A bull will be worth so much money, but a horse will be worth only a few silver coins.

For three years before the Anti-Christ emerges, the people will suffer severe hunger. In the first year, Allah will order the sky to withhold a third of its rain, and the earth to withhold one-third of its crops. In the second year, He will order the sky to withhold two-thirds of its rain, and the earth to withhold two-thirds of its crops. In the third year, He will order the sky to withhold all of its rain so not even a drop will fall, and the earth to withhold all of its crops, so that nothing green will grow. Every cloven-hoofed creature will die except for whatever Allah wills."

Someone asked, "How will the people live at that time?" He said, "By saying La illaha illa Allah (There is nothing worthy of worship except God), Allahu Akbar (God is greater), Subhan Allah (How perfect is God) and Al-Hamdulillah (All praise belongs to God). This will be like food for them." (Albaani - Saheeh al-Jaami')

The people of the Prophet Jesus were well known for their knowledge of medicine. He was aided with miracles that his people could comprehend.

07 MIRACLES OF PROPHET JESUS

At times people would reject the veracity of a Prophet and would not believe until they witnessed a tangible miracle. So in light of this, Allah sent his Prophets and Messengers with miracles. Allah, the Exalted, says:

"And We have already sent messengers before you and assigned to them wives and descendants. And it was not for a messenger to come with a sign except by permission of Allah. For every term is a decree." (Qur'an 13:38)

Another miracle Prophet Jesus received was the Feast. His disciples asked for a heavenly feast so that their hearts would be affirmed.

Each prophet was given miracles that their nations could both relate to and comprehend. The people of the Prophet Moses were well known for their mastery of sorcery. So Allah aided the Prophet Moses with miracles his people could comprehend; his staff miraculously transformed into a serpent. God, the Exalted, says:

"And the magicians came to Pharaoh. They said, 'Certainly there will be for us a reward if we are the victorious?' He said, 'Yes, and [moreover], you will be among those made near [to me].' They said, 'O Moses, either you throw [down your staff], or we will be the ones to throw [first].' He said, 'Throw,' and when they threw, they bewitched the eyes of the people and struck terror into them, and they presented a great [feat of] magic. And We inspired to Moses, 'Throw your staff,' and at once it devoured what they were falsifying. So the truth was established, and abolished was what they were doing. And Pharaoh and his people were overcome right there and became debased. And the magicians fell down in prostration [to Allah]. They said, 'We have believed in the Lord of the worlds. The Lord of Moses and Aaron.'" (Qur'an 7:113-121)

Conversely, the people of the Prophet Jesus were well known for their knowledge of medicine. He was aided with miracles that his people could comprehend. He spoke to people while he was a newborn infant. He would make a bird's shape in clay, and then by the will of God, life would be breathed into it. He would heal, by the will of God, the lepers and those who were blind. He even, by the will of God, brought the dead back to life. God says:
"[The Day] when God will say, 'O Jesus, Son of Mary, remember My favor upon you and upon your mother when I supported you with the Holy Spirit and you spoke to the people in the cradle and [later] in maturity. And [remember] when I taught you writing and wisdom, and the Torah and the Gospel. And when you designed from clay the likeness of a bird with My permission, then you breathed into it, and it became a bird with My permission. And you healed the blind and the leper with My permission. And when you brought forth the dead with My permission. And when I restrained the Children of Israel from [killing] you when you came to them with clear proofs and those who disbelieved among them said, 'This is not but obvious magic.'" (Qur'an 5:110)

Another miracle Prophet Jesus received was the Feast. His disciples asked for a heavenly feast so that their hearts would be reassured in faith. So he prayed to Allah for this, and it was granted. Allah, the Exalted, says:
"[And remember] when the disciples said, 'O Jesus, Son of Mary, can your Lord send down to us a table [spread with food] from the heaven?' [Jesus] replied, 'Fear God, if you are believers.' They said, 'We wish to eat from it and let our hearts be reassured and know that you have been truthful to us, and so that we may be among its witnesses.'" (Qur'an 5:112-113)

08 THE PROPHET JESUS AND HIS REJECTION OF SHIRK (POLYTHEISM)

The Qur'an has mentioned to us that Jesus was like all Prophets and Messengers sent by God. He upheld the belief in the Oneness of Allah. God, the Exalted, says:

"And when Jesus brought clear proofs, he said, 'I have come to you with wisdom and to make clear to you some of that over which you differ, so fear God and obey me. Indeed, God is my Lord and your Lord, so worship Him. This is a straight path.'" (Qur'an 43:63-64)

The Qur'an has mentioned to us that Jesus was like all Prophets and Messengers sent by God. He upheld the belief in the Oneness of God.

The Qur'an clarifies that Jesus never called for people to worship him. God, the Exalted, says:

"And [beware the Day] when God will say, 'O Jesus son of Mary, did you say to the people, 'Take me and my mother as deities besides Allah?' He will say, 'Exalted are You! It was not for me to say that to which I have no right. If I had said it, You would have known it. You know what is within myself, and I do not know what is within Yourself. Indeed, it is You who is the Knower of the unseen. I only said to them what You commanded me - to worship Allah, my Lord and your Lord. And I was a witness over them as long as I was among them. But when You took me up, You were the Observer over them, and You are, over all things, Witness. If You should punish them, indeed they are Your servants. But if You forgive them, indeed it is You who is the Exalted in Might, the Wise.'" (Qur'an 5:116-118)

The Prophet Jesus asked his people to believe in the Messenger to come, the Prophet Muhammad.

09 THE GLAD TIDINGS OF PROPHET JESUS OF THE ADVENT OF PROPHET MUHAMMAD

The Message of every Prophet was identical in matters of creedal belief. God, the Exalted, says:

"And recall, O People of the Scripture, when God took the covenant of the prophets, saying, 'Whatever I give you of the Scripture and wisdom, and then there comes to you a messenger confirming what is with you, you [must] believe in him and support him.' God said, 'Have you acknowledged and taken upon that My commitment?' They said, 'We have acknowledged it.' He said, 'Then bear witness, and I am with you among the witnesses.' And whoever turned away after that - they were the defiantly disobedient." (Qur'an 3:81-82)

The Prophet Jesus asked his people to believe in the Messenger to come, the Prophet Muhammad. God, the Exalted, says:
"O Children of Israel, remember My favor which I have bestowed upon you and fulfill My covenant [upon you] and I will fulfill your covenant with Me, and be afraid of only Me. And believe in what I have sent down confirming that which is already with you, and be not the first to disbelieve in it. And do not exchange My signs for a small price, and fear only Me. And do not mix the truth with falsehood or conceal the truth while you know it." (Qur'an 2:40-42)

Jesus Christ was one more prophet in the long line of prophets sent to the Children of Israel. It is recorded in the Bible that he said:
"I was sent only to the lost sheep of Israel." (Matthew 15:24)

When Jesus sent the disciples out in the path of God, he instructed them:
"Do not go into the way of the Gentiles, and do not enter a city of the Samaritans. But go rather to the lost sheep of the house of Israel." (Matthew 10:5-6)

Throughout his ministry, Jesus was never recorded as having converted a Gentile, and in fact is recorded as having initially rebuked a Gentile for seeking his favors, likening her to a dog (Matthew 15:22-28 and Mark 7:25-30).

Jesus was himself a Jew, his disciples were Jews, and both he and they directed their ministries to the Jews. One wonders what this means to us now, for most of those who have taken Jesus as their "personal savior" are Gentiles, and not of the "lost sheep of the house of Israel" to whom he was sent!

From this passage we also learn that Jesus was not sent to mankind at large. God, the Exalted, says:
"And [mention] when Jesus the son of Mary, said, 'O children of Israel, indeed I am the messenger of God to you confirming what came before me of the Torah and bringing good tidings of a messenger, to come after me, whose name is Ahmad.' But when he came to them with clear evidences, they said, 'This is obvious sorcery.'" (Qur'an 61:6)

10 THE POSITION OF THE RABBIS AND PRIESTS TOWARDS PROPHET MUHAMMAD ﷺ

The Priests and Rabbis who had heard of the Message of the Prophet Muhammad knew that it was the truth, for details of his life are mentioned in the previous scriptures. God, the Exalted, says:

"Those who follow the Messenger, the unlettered prophet, whom they find written in what they have of the Torah and the Gospel, who enjoins upon them what is right and forbids them what is wrong and makes lawful for them the good things and prohibits for them the evil and relieves them of their burden and the shackles which were upon them. So they who have believed in him, honored him, supported him and followed the light which was sent down with him; it is those who will be the successful." (Qur'an 7:157)

Safiyah, the daughter of the Jewish Noble Ka'b, said: "My father and my uncle, Abu Yasir, went to visit the Messenger of Allah and returned towards the end of that day, exhausted and tired. I tried to cheer them up, but they didn't look at me. I heard my uncle ask my father, 'Is it him?' I heard him say, 'By the Lord of Moses, it is!' My uncle then asked, 'What shall we do?' He said, 'I will be an enemy to him till death.'"

Many accepted the Message of Islam, and amongst them was the King of Ethiopia, the Negus. He was a Christian and was very knowledgeable regarding the Scripture. He knew that a Prophet would come after Jesus. Umm Salamah said, "When we arrived in the land of Ethiopia, the Negus was very kind to us. He gave us protection and allowed us freedom to worship God alone. We were not harmed in any way."

Quraish could not tolerate the prospect of a secure haven available for the Muslims in Abyssinia (Ethiopia), so they dispatched two envoys to demand the extradition of the Muslims. They were 'Amr bin Al-'As and 'Abdullah bin Abi Rabi'a - before they would embrace Islam years later. They had taken with them valuable gifts to the king and his clergy, and had been able to win some of the courtiers over to their side. The pagan envoys claimed that the Muslim refugees should be expelled from Abyssinia (Ethiopia) and be handed over to

Many accepted the Message of Islam, and amongst them was the King of Ethiopia, the Negus.

Quraish could not tolerate the prospect of a secure haven available for the Muslims in Abyssinia (Ethiopia), so they dispatched two envoys to demand the extradition of the Muslims.

them, on the grounds that they had abandoned the religion of their forefathers, and that their leader was preaching a religion different from theirs and from that of the king.

The king summoned the Muslims to the court and asked them to explain the teachings of their religion. The Muslim emigrants had decided to tell the whole truth, with no regard to the possible consequences. Ja'far bin Abi Talib stood up and addressed the king in the following words:

"O King! We were a people plunged in the depths of ignorance and barbarism. We adored idols, we lived unchastely, we ate carrion, and we spoke in a most vile manner. We disregarded ties of mutual respect and the duties of hospitality and neighborhood. We knew no law but that of the strong [devours the weak].

Allah then raised from among us a man, whose truthfulness, honesty, and purity we knew well. He called us to the Oneness of God, and taught us not to associate anything with Him. He forbade us from the worship of idols, and he enjoined us to speak the truth, to be faithful to our trusts, to be merciful and to uphold the rights of the neighbors and the kith and kin. He forbade us to speak evil of women, or to steal the wealth of orphans. In short, he ordered us to refrain from all evil.

He ordered us to offer prayers, to give charity to the poor and needy, and to observe fasting. We have believed in him, we have accepted his teachings and his injunctions to worship God, and not to associate anything with Him, and we have allowed what He has allowed, and prohibited what He has prohibited.

For this reason, our people have risen against us, have persecuted us in order to make us forsake the worship of God and return to the worship of idols and other abominations. They have tortured and harmed us, so we came to your country so that we would be safe."

The King was very impressed by these words and asked the Muslims to recite some of Allah's Revelation. Ja'far recited the opening verses of Surah Maryam (Chapter 19 Mary). In this chapter, God speaks of the birth of the Prophet Jesus. Thereupon the King, along with the bishops, was moved to tears. The Negus exclaimed, "It seems as if these words and those which were revealed to Jesus are rays of light that have radiated from the same source."

Turning to the envoys of Quraish, he said, "I will not give them up! They are free to live and worship in my kingdom as they please."

Umm Salamah said: "When we arrived in the land of Ethiopia, the Negus was very kind to us. He gave us protection and allowed us freedom to worship Allah alone."

The next day, the envoys went to the King and said that Muhammad ﷺ and his followers claimed that Jesus was not the son of God. Again the Muslims were summoned and asked regarding their belief in Jesus.

Ja'far again stood up and replied: "We speak about Jesus as we have been taught by our Prophet ﷺ. That is, he is the servant of God, His Messenger, and that he was created by the command of God." The king at once remarked, "We believe the same! Blessed be you, and blessed be your master."

Some of the ministers became upset, so he said to them, "You may fume as you like, but Jesus is nothing more than what Ja'far has said about him." He then assured the Muslims of his full protection. He returned the gifts he had been given by Quraish. The Muslims lived in Abyssinia (Ethiopia) for a number of years till they returned to Madinah.[1]

Another inspiring story is one that took place between some of the Quraish traders and King Heraclius of Rome.

The Negus exclaimed: "It seems as if these words and those which were revealed to Jesus are rays of light that have radiated from the same source."

Abdullah b. Abbas, the nephew of the Prophet, reported that the Messenger of God ﷺ wrote to Heraclius and invited him to Islam though a letter he sent with a companion of his named Dihya al-Kalbi. Dihya handed this letter to the Governor of Basra who then forwarded it to Heraclius.

Heraclius, as a sign of gratitude to God, had walked from Aleppo to Jerusalem when God had granted Him victory over the Persian forces. When the letter of the Messenger of God reached Heraclius, he said after reading it, "Seek for me anyone from among his people if they are present here, in order to ask them about the Messenger of God!"

(1) Ibn Hisham 1/334-338

At that time, Abu Sufyan bin Harb was in the Greater Syria Area[1] with some men from Quraish who had come as merchants during the truce that had been concluded between the Messenger of God and the pagans of Quraish. Abu Sufyan said,

"Heraclius' messenger found us somewhere in the Greater Syria area, so he took me and my companions to Jerusalem and we were admitted into Heraclius' presence. We found him sitting in his royal court wearing a crown, surrounded by the senior Byzantine dignitaries. He said to his translator, 'Ask them whom amongst them is a close relation to the man who claims to be a prophet.'"

Abu Sufyan added, "I replied, 'I am the nearest relative to him.' He asked, 'What degree of relationship do you have with him?' I replied, 'He is my cousin,' and there was none from the tribe of Abd Manaf in the caravan except myself.

Heraclius said, 'Let him come nearer.' He then ordered that my companions stand behind me near my shoulder and said to his translator, 'Tell his companions that I am going to ask this man about the one who claims to be a prophet. If he tells a lie, they should contradict him immediately.'"

Abu Sufyan added, "By Allah! Had it not been for shame that my companions brand me a liar, I would not have spoken the truth about him when he asked me. But I considered it shameful to be called a liar by my companions, so I told the truth."

"He then said to his translator, 'Ask him what kind of family he belongs to.' I replied, 'He belongs to a noble family amongst us.' He asked, 'Has anybody else amongst you ever claimed the same before him?' I replied, 'No.' He asked, 'Have you ever blamed him for telling lies before he claimed what he claimed?' I replied, 'No.' He asked, 'Was anybody amongst his ancestors a king?' I replied, 'No.' He asked, 'Do the noble or the poor follow him?' I replied, 'It is the poor who follow him.' He asked, 'Are they increasing or decreasing (daily)?' I replied, 'They are increasing.' He asked, 'Does anybody amongst those who embrace his religion become displeased and then discard his religion?' I replied, 'No.' He asked, 'Does he break his promises?' I replied, 'No, but we are now at truce with him and we are afraid that he may betray us.'"

(1) This is a historic region in the Middle East bordering the Mediterranean. It is generally considered to include the modern states of Syria, Lebanon, Palestine, and Jordan.

Abu Sufyan added, "Other than the last sentence, I could not say anything against him."

"Heraclius then asked, 'Have you ever had a war with him?' I replied, 'Yes.' He asked, 'What was the outcome of your battles with him?' I replied, 'Sometimes he was victorious and sometimes we.' He asked, 'What does he order you to do?' I said, 'He tells us to worship God alone, and not to worship others along with Him, and to leave all that our forefathers used to worship. He orders us to pray, give in charity, be chaste, keep promises and return what is entrusted to us.'

When I had said that, Heraclius said to his translator, 'Say to him, 'I asked you about his lineage and your reply was that he belonged to a noble family. In fact, all the Messengers came from the noblest lineage of their nations. Then I questioned you whether anybody else amongst you had claimed such a thing, and your reply was in the negative. If the answer had been in the affirmative, I would have thought that this man was following a claim that had been said before him. When I asked you whether he was ever blamed for telling lies, your reply was in the negative, so I assume that a person who did not tell a lie to people could never tell a lie about God. Then I asked you whether any of his ancestors was a king. Your reply was in the negative, and if it had been in the affirmative, I would have thought that this man wanted to take back his ancestral kingdom. When I asked you whether the rich or the poor people followed him, you replied that it was the poor who followed him. In fact, such are the followers of the Messengers. Then I asked you whether his followers were increasing or decreasing. You replied that they were increasing. In fact, this is the result of true faith till it is complete. I asked you whether there was anybody who, after embracing his religion, became displeased and discarded his religion. Your reply was in the negative. In fact, this is the sign of true faith, for when its pleasure enters and mixes in the hearts completely; nobody will be displeased with it. I asked you whether he had ever broken his promise. You replied in the negative. And such are the Messengers; they never break their promises. When I asked you whether you fought with him and he fought with you, you replied that he did and that sometimes he was victorious and sometimes you. Indeed, such are the Messengers; they are put to trials, yet the final victory is always theirs. Then I asked you what he ordered you. You replied that he ordered you to worship God alone and not to worship others along with Him, to leave all that your forefathers used to worship, to offer prayers, to speak the truth, to be chaste, to keep promises, and to return what is entrusted to you. These are really the qualities of a prophet, who I knew [from the previous Scriptures] would appear, but I did not know that he would be from amongst you. If what you say is true, he will very soon occupy the earth under my feet, and if I knew that I would reach him definitely, I would go immediately to meet him. And were I with him, then I would certainly wash his feet.'"

Abu Sufyan added, "Heraclius then asked for the letter of the Messenger of God and it was read. Its contents were the following:
'I begin with the name of Allah, the most Beneficent, the most Merciful. This letter is from Muhammad, the servant of God and His Messenger, to Heraclius, the Byzantine Ruler. Peace be upon the followers of guidance. I invite you to accept Islam. Accept Islam and you will be safe. Accept Islam and God will bestow on you a double reward. But if you reject this invitation of Islam, you shall be responsible for misguiding the people of your nation.

'Say, 'O People of the Scripture, come to a word that is equitable between us and you - that we will not worship except Allah and not associate anything with Him and not take one another as lords instead of Allah.' But if they turn away, then say, 'Bear witness that we are Muslims [submitting to Him].'" (Qur'an 3:64)

Abu Sufyan added, "When Heraclius had finished his speech, there was a great hue and cry caused by the Byzantine dignitaries surrounding him, and there was so much noise that I did not understand what they said. So, we were ordered out of the court.

When I went out with my companions and we were alone, I said to them, 'Verily, [Muhammad's] affair has indeed gained power. This is the King of the Romans fearing him.'"

Abu Sufyan added, "By God, I became surer and surer that his religion would be victorious till I ultimately accepted Islam." (Bukhari #2782)

The Prophet Muhammad ﷺ also invited the Christians of the Southern Arabian region of Najran to embrace Islam. The Christians counseled among themselves and decided to send a group of their scholars to meet the Prophet.

Allah describes the true followers of Jesus as being among those who rush to accept the truth and follow it whole-heartedly.

Upon meeting them, the Prophet ﷺ preached to them and requested them to accept Islam. They asked, "What is your opinion about Jesus?" The Prophet ﷺ said, "Take a rest today and you will receive the replies to all your questions." The Prophet ﷺ was awaiting a revelation in this matter, and the next day the verses 59-60 from the third chapter were revealed to him.

"To God, the case of Jesus is as that of Adam, whom He created from the earth and then said, 'Exist,' and Adam came into existence. The truth is from your Lord, so do not be among the doubters." (Qur'an 3:59-60)

The next day, when the Christians came before the Prophet ﷺ he recited to them the verses that were revealed to him. Despite what they heard, they refused to accept the truth. Thus verse 61 was revealed from the same chapter.

The Muslim belief in relation to the Prophet Jesus is that he was not killed, nor crucified. Rather, he ascended into the Heavens by the will of God.

"Then whoever argues with you about it after this knowledge has come to you, say to them, 'Come, let us call our sons and your sons, our women and your women, ourselves and yourselves, then supplicate earnestly [together] and invoke the curse of God upon the liars [among us].'" (Qur'an 3:61)

With this the Prophet ﷺ challenged them to "Mubahala", which means to invoke a curse upon the lying party. The Christian delegation consulted each other and ultimately announced their acceptance of the challenge. Early the next morning, the Prophet ﷺ sent Salman al-Farsi to an open place, fixed outside the city for the historic event. When the Christians of Najran saw the Prophet ﷺ, they were awestruck and spellbound.

Al-'Aqib and As-Saiyid, two of the chiefs of the Christian delegation, said to each other:

"We shall not supplicate. For, I swear by God, if he is really a Prophet and exchanges curses with us, we will never prosper, nor will our descendants. Consequently neither we, nor our animals will survive it."

In the end, they decided to resort to the Messenger of Allah's judgment about their cause. They came to him and stated that though they would not accept Islam, they would accept the protection and rule of the Islamic government over their territories. The Messenger of Allah then offered them to pay tribute and he made peace with them. In return, they were under the covenant of Allah and His Messenger that afforded them protection and the freedom to practice their religious affairs freely.

THE CHARACTERISTICS OF THE FOLLOWERS OF JESUS

Allah describes them in the Qur'an, saying:
"Then We sent following their footsteps Our messengers and followed [them] with Jesus the son of Mary, and gave him the Gospel. And We placed in the hearts of those who followed him compassion and mercy. And monasticism, which they innovated, We did not prescribe it for them except that they did so seeking the approval of Allah. But they did not observe it with due observance. So We gave the ones who believed among them their reward, but many of them are defiantly disobedient." (Qur'an 57:27)

Allah describes the true followers of Jesus as being among those who rush to accept the truth and follow it whole-heartedly. They work to spread the true message of Jesus. Allah has ordered the Muslims to follow suit and be like the followers of Jesus. He says:
"O you who have believed, be supporters of Allah, as when Jesus the son of Mary, said to the disciples, 'Who are my supporters for Allah?' The disciples said, 'We are supporters of Allah.' And a faction of the Children of Israel believed

and a faction disbelieved. So We supported those who believed against their enemy, and they became dominant." (Qur'an 61:14)

Allah also describes them as being the closest of people to the Muslims. He says:

"You will find the nearest of people in affection to the believers those who say, 'We are Christians.' That is because among them are priests and monks and because they are not arrogant. And when they hear what has been revealed to the Messenger, you see their eyes overflowing with tears because of what they have recognized of the truth. They say, 'Our Lord, we have believed, so count us among the witnesses.'" (Qur'an 5:82-83)

As Muslims, we believe that every one of us will stand before God to be judged for what they have done. No one bears the sins of anyone else.

12 THE ASCENSION OF THE PROPHET JESUS INTO THE HEAVENS

The Muslim belief in relation to the Prophet Jesus is that he was not killed, nor crucified. Rather, that God saved him from the plots of those who wanted to kill him, and took him up into the Heavens by the will of God. Allah, the Exalted, says:

"... And We gave Jesus the son of Mary, clear proofs and supported him with the Holy Spirit. But is it not that every time a messenger came to you, [O Children of Israel], with what your souls did not desire, you were arrogant? And a group [of messengers] you denied and another group you killed." (Qur'an 2:87)

Muslims believe that the Prophet Jesus will return to earth towards the end of time. He will return during a period in which ignorance would become widespread and people would be distanced from Faith.

God, the Exalted, also says:

"And [We cursed them] for their breaking of the covenant and their disbelief in the signs of Allah and their killing of the prophets without right, and their saying, 'Our hearts are wrapped'. Rather, Allah has sealed them because of their disbelief, so they believe not, except for a few.

And [We cursed them] for their disbelief and their saying against Mary a great slander, and [for] their saying, 'Indeed, we have killed the Messiah, Jesus the son of Mary, the messenger of Allah.' And they did not kill him, nor did they crucify him, but another was made to resemble him to them. And indeed, those who differ over it are in doubt about it. They have no knowledge of it except the following of assumption.

And they did not kill him, for certain. Rather, Allah raised him to Himself. And ever is Allah Exalted in Might and Wise. And there is none from the People of the Scripture but that he will surely believe in Jesus before his death. And on the Day of Resurrection he will be against them a witness." (Qur'an 4:155-159)

Ibn Kathir records in his commentary on the Qur'an: "When Allah sent Jesus with proofs and guidance, the Jews envied him because of his prophethood and obvious miracles; curing the blind and leprous and bringing the dead back to life, by Allah's permission. He also used to make the shape of a bird from clay and blow in it, and it became a bird by Allah's permission and flew. Jesus performed other miracles that Allah honored him with, yet the Jews defied and belied him and tried their best to harm him. The Prophet Jesus could not live in any one city for long, and he had to travel often with his mother, peace be upon them.

Even so, the Jews were not satisfied, and they went to the King of Damascus at that time, a Greek polytheist who worshipped the stars. They told him that there was a man in Jerusalem misguiding and dividing the people in Jerusalem and stirring unrest among the King's subjects.

The King became angry and wrote to his deputy in Jerusalem to arrest the rebel leader, stop him from causing unrest, crucify him and make him wear a crown of thorns. When the King's deputy in Jerusalem received these orders, he went with some Jews to the house that Jesus was residing in, and he was then with twelve, thirteen or seventeen of his disciples. That day was a Friday, in the evening.

They surrounded Jesus in the house, and when he felt that they would soon enter the house, he said to his companions, 'Who volunteers to be made to look like me, for which he will be my companion in Paradise?' A young man volunteered, but Jesus thought that he was too young. He asked the question a second and third time, and each time the young man volunteered while the others remained quiet. This prompted Jesus to say, 'You will be that man.' Allah made the young man to look exactly like Jesus, and a hole opened in the roof of the house, and Jesus was made to sleep and ascended to heaven while asleep." (Tafsir Ibn Kathir)

Jesus is not as the Christians assert; a Son of God or part of the Trinity. He is only a Messenger of God sent to his people to convey to them the belief in the Oneness of God.

God, the Exalted, says:

"And the disbelievers planned, but Allah planned. And Allah is the best of planners. [Mention] when Allah said, 'O Jesus, indeed I will take you and raise you to Myself and purify you from those who disbelieve and make those who follow you [in submission to Allah alone] superior to those who disbelieve until the Day of Resurrection. Then to Me is your return, and I will judge between you concerning that in which you used to differ. And as for those who disbelieved, I will punish them with a severe punishment in this world and the Hereafter, and they will have no helpers.' But as for those who believed and did righteous deeds, He will give them in full their rewards, and Allah does not like the wrongdoers." (Qur'an 3:54-57)

Christians later claimed that Jesus was killed to atone for the sins of mankind. As Muslims, we believe that every one of us will stand before God to be judged for what they have done. No one bears the sins of anyone else.

In conclusion, we extend our hands to the People of the Book and ask them to read intellectually their own books and to ask questions, to seek knowledge and search sincerely for the truth.

13 THE DESCENT OF THE PROPHET JESUS

Muslims believe that the Prophet Jesus will return to earth towards the end of time. He will return during a period in which ignorance would become widespread and people would be distanced from Faith. The Prophet Jesus will be a just ruler who will rule by the laws of Islam.

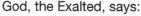

CONCLUSION

There has been a great amount of dispute about the Prophet Jesus. Some despised him and ascribed to him the worst of descriptions, and there were others who adulated him so much that it led them to worship him. God guided the Muslims to the moderate and balanced path. We recognize the greatness of this noble Prophet of God. We love, respect and revere him, but we do not worship him. He is indeed a great messenger of God, but he is only a man who has no claim to divinity. This is what we find affirmed in the Qur'an and the Prophetic Traditions. Jesus is not as the Christians assert; a Son of God or part of the Trinity. He is only a Messenger of God sent to his people to convey to them the belief in the Oneness of God.

God has blessed us with the faculty of reason and intellect. We have to use this to discern who deserves worship and who does not.

In conclusion, we extend our hands to the People of the Book and ask them to read intellectually their own books and to ask questions, to seek knowledge and search sincerely for the truth. God, the Exalted, says:
"And if you obey most of those upon the earth, they will mislead you from the way of Allah. They follow not except assumption, and they are not but falsifying." (Qur'an 6:116)

The Jews and the Christians were given the glad tidings of a Prophet to come. They thought he would be from the Children of Israel, but when he came from amongst those other than them, they disbelieved in him. God says:
"And when there came to them a Book from God confirming that which was with them, although before they used to pray for victory against those who disbelieved, but [then] when there came to them that which they recognized, they disbelieved in it. So the curse of God will be upon the disbelievers." (Qur'an 2:89)

I hope that this book will serve as an eye-opener for you and act as the beginning of your journey in the search for the truth. The beauty of the truth is that once you have it, and cling to it, you will find peace and tranquility. God, the Exalted, says:
"Those who have believed and whose hearts are assured by the remembrance of Allah. Unquestionably, by the remembrance of Allah hearts are assured." (Qur'an 13:28)

THE MESSENGER OF GOD MUHAMMAD

An account of the life of Prophet Muhammad (peace be upon him). The book introduces us to the Prophet's noble character, his humble life and his conduct with his family at home, his companions and all people in society. It tells us how he strove to fulfil the task God assigned to him and contemplates how he dealt with his enemies, the exceptional magnanimity he showed to all and his simple, but highly effective, method of advocating his message.

THE KEY TO UNDERSTANDING ISLAM

This book explains how Islam is a code of living that covers all aspects of life. It comprises a set of acts of worship which play important roles in placing morality on a solid foundation and strengthening good qualities in people so that they are keen to follow the right path. The book cites many examples and speaks about the importance Islam attaches to knowledge. It mentions a number of recent scientific discoveries that the Qur'an has referred to 14 centuries ago.

MESSAGE OF ISLAM

The Message of Islam begins by reminding the reader that Islam, its worship, the rules governing people's transactions and all its teachings have always remained the same as they were taught by Prophet Muhammad (peace be upon him). No change or alteration has been introduced into the religion, though some Muslims have changed. The book discusses and sheds light on a number of rights to which Islam attaches great importance.

ISLAM IS THE RELIGION OF PEACE

Islam is the Religion of Peace, shows with perfect clarity that Islam is the religion of peace and that the spread of Islam means the spread of peace throughout the world. Muslims must always be true to their promises and covenants and treat others with justice and compassion.

EASE AND TOLERANCE IN ISLAM

This book explains that Islam admits no rigidity and making things easy is a general feature of all aspects of the Islamic faith. It is a religion God revealed that can be implemented by people with different failings, feelings and abilities. Islamic law takes all this into account and addresses human nature and appeals to it. God says: "He has laid no hardship on you in anything that pertains to religion." (22: 78)

HUMAN RIGHTS IN ISLAM

Human rights in Islam are outlined in the Qur'an and the teachings of Prophet Muhammad (peace be upon him). They aim to make man lead a life of compassion and dignity, so that he acquires all good qualities and deals with others in the best manner. The book clarifies the misconceptions that are often expressed regarding the different aspects of freedom and responds to criticism in a calm and objective way.

BILAL THE ABYSSINIAN

This book tells the history of Bilal ibn Rabah, a former slave who became a companion of the Prophet. The book expounds Islam's attitude to racial discrimination, highlighting significant events that show the Prophet took care of many of those who were persecuted, protected them and gave them their rightful status in the Muslim community.

THE PATH TO HAPPINESS

The Path to Happiness explains that the way of life Islam provides for its followers is divine and intended to ensure that people enjoy real happiness in this present life and in the life to come. Islam establishes the concept of true and everlasting happiness, which makes Muslims aspire to the sublime through obedience of God and earning His pleasure.

WOMEN IN ISLAM

This book discusses the status of women prior to Islam and how women were ill-treated and humiliated in many cultures. It explains how Islam put an end to all this injustice, established women's rights and gave women their rightful status.

ROMANCE IN ISLAM

This book highlights the great importance Islam attaches to love. It shows that the love of God is the best and the most noble love. When it is rooted in a person's heart, it sets that person's behaviour on the right footing, elevates his emotions and feelings and removes selfishness. A person who truly loves God extends feelings of love and compassion to all creatures.

ISLAMIC PERSPECTIVE ON SEX

This book discusses the Islamic approach to sex and how to satisfy the sexual desire in the proper and beneficial way. The proper way to satisfy sexual desire is within marriage and according to Islam, marriage is a necessity for the individual to achieve personal fulfilment. For society, marriage is the way to progress, development and stability.

JESUS IN THE QURAN

After first discussing people's need to receive the divine message through prophets, this book relates the story of Jesus, son of Mary (peace be upon him). It starts well before his birth, then goes on to discuss his message and the opposition he had to endure. The book also discusses the Qur'anic account of Jesus, which makes clear that he enjoys a very high position with God Almighty.

GLAD TIDINGS

Glad Tidings explains the nature of Islam and clarifies the error of people who rely for information on suspect sources. The book highlights the main features of Islam and tells everyone who embraces Islam that God erases all their past sins and errors. As the Prophet makes clear: "Islam wipes away all past sins."

MY FIRST STEPS IN ISLAM

This book explains for non-Muslim readers how to embrace Islam and shows that this does not require much effort. To new Muslims, the book explains the essential elements of Islam and outlines the character of Prophet Muhammad, his qualities and the message he delivered to mankind. It goes on to discuss the various acts of worship Muslims are required to offer, as well as their purposes and significance.

THE PURITY

Under Islam, the concept of purification is not limited to personal and physical purity; it includes purifying oneself of sin and all disobedience of God. This book discusses the detailed rules of physical purification, including ablution, grand ablution, the removal of impurity, dry ablution, etc.

HISN AL-MU'MIN

Hisn Al-Mu'min speaks of the causes of reversals and misfortunes that people encounter. It highlights how one can ensure the protection and preservation of God's favours and blessings, as well as preventing harm and reducing the effects of personal tragedies and calamities. The book teaches the ways and means to fortify oneself against the effect of such tragedies, the most important being remembrance of God and glorifying Him at all times. This book explains the best forms of such remembrance and glorification.

THE BEGINNING AND THE END

Questions of the creation, existence and progress of the universe have been raised by communities throughout the ages. Yet from its earliest days, Islam addressed these questions in a most direct and clear way. This book explains that the ultimate objective of creation is for all creatures to submit themselves to God and worship Him alone. All aspects of life in the universe inevitably end in death then will be brought back to life on the Day of Resurrection when they receive due recompense for their actions.

EVERY RELIGIOUS INNOVATION

This book defines and explains the various types of deviation from the essence of Islam and its true teachings. It reveals the negative consequences of deviation on Muslims and their life and how deviation is bound to give non-Muslims a distorted view of Islam. Finally, the book describes the role of Muslims in discarding all deviation, according to their abilities.

Osoul Center
www.osoulcenter.com

IslamHouse.com

eDialogue

Interested in ISLAM?
Join For a Free Private Live Chat

edialogue org

For more details visit
www.GuideToIslam.com

GUIDE TO
ISLAM

contact us :Books@guidetoislam.com

JESUS
N THE QURAN

d's messengers and prophets are assigned the task of giving people the right concept God, their Creator, and this book speaks first about people's need to receive the divine ssage through prophets. It explains how prophets taught people how to earn His pleas- and acceptance and how to avoid incurring His anger. They put this into practice, so t their teachings would serve as a code by which to live, setting human life on the t course and ensuring happiness in the life to come.

book relates the story of Jesus, son of Mary (peace be upon), starting when his virtuous mother was pregnant, then scribing his birth, his message and the opposition he to endure. The author then discusses the 'anic account of Jesus, which makes clear he enjoys a very high position with God ighty.

trust that you will enjoy reading book and we will be happy receive your comments observations.

ISBN: 978-6039093602

9 786039 093602

Downlad the book

www.guidetolslam.com

Osoul Center

Lightning Source UK Ltd.
Milton Keynes UK
UKHW020321200123
415634UK00002B/21

9 780368 646287